Books by Barbara Rose PhD

Signs of Men Who Cannot Fully Love—
Why & How to Understand It (Pocket Coach Series)

How to Get OVER AN EX When You're
Still in Love (Pocket Coach Series)

Essential Custody Guidelines for Britney Spears

Your Loved One JUST Visited You:
Solace After the Passing of a Loved One

The Messiah's Handbook

High Self Esteem

Tempted by Death: Why Suicide Cannot be an Option

Soulmates Courtship with Destiny

Being an Adult Child of Parental Alienation Syndrome

The Complete Guide to Your Soul Mate Relationship

The Rush to Spend

BARBARA ROSE, PhD

BARBARA ROSE, PhD
BORN TO INSPIRE

LOVE

THE 10

AGREEMENTS

THE GUIDE TO PROPEL YOU AND YOUR ROMANTIC RELATIONSHIP TO EXTRAORDINARY HEIGHTS

THE ROSE GROUP
Uplifting Humanity One Book at a Time ™

THE TEN LOVE AGREEMENTS:
The Guide to Propel You and Your Romantic
Relationship to Extraordinary Heights

ISBN-10: 0-9908138-4-3
ISBN-13: 978-0-9908138-4-2

Cover art and interior book design by: Greg Traver at Command G Design Group. *www.commandgdesign.com*

You may contact the author through her Web site:
https://BornToInspire.com

Subject Classification:
Books > Relationships > Love and Romance
Books > Relationships > Marriage and Long Term Relationships
Books > Spirituality > Personal Transformation and Spirituality
Authors, A—Z > Rose, Barbara

CONTENTS

CHAPTER 1

&

THE LOVE AGREEMENT
FOR HONESTY

One of the most crucial aspects of your romantic relationship is honesty. Being completely transparent with your partner will enable you to be fully yourself. This creates a trusting bond that will enable your life-long partnership to flourish. Let's face it: only when you're 100 percent honest with yourself can you have the capacity to share your truth with the one you love. It takes a lot of courage to be completely honest with yourself—especially concerning any doubts and insecurities you may have hidden at the soul level.

Perhaps you fear that revealing those areas you would rather push down would cause your loved one to run for their life. This is actually the farthest from the truth. You see, when you can bare your soul first to yourself and then to your loved one, what is actually created is deep intimacy—the cornerstone of a profound love relationship.

Yes, it feels scary, as if you're about to jump off a cliff, but it is that precise fear of revealing the areas of

1

relationship fear, self-put-downs, past trauma, and all insecurities you have that is the catalyst to uprooting those fears. Only once they've been resolved will you finally feel loved despite them and finally come to a place of inner acceptance that paves the way for unprecedented personal transformation and profound relationship growth.

How can you know if you are pushing your fears down? You feel scared to death to expose them! When you feel deep fear, this is your light bulb to let you know that this particular area is in dire need of transformation once and for all.

It is time for you to be *free* of your fears, and the only way to free yourself from them is to expose them from the bottom of your heart with the earnest desire to transform them.

This is the opposite of complaining about yourself. It is a deep resolution that you have finally mustered up the courage to evolve from the old fears, and this takes a lot of guts. It will take you out of your comfort zone, and you might think you have to put on an act to appear perfect. But because no one is perfect, everyone needs to evolve on the soul level, so you are not alone.

When you truly desire to evolve into the absolute best you can be, it will require you to be boldly honest, sharing from the core of your heart precisely those areas you wish you never felt, first to yourself and then to your partner. Then guess what will happen? When you share your deepest fears and insecurities because you genuinely want them to be completely behind you, you are paving the way for you to leave them behind. This is enormous growth! You may have had these issues for eons. Perhaps you have had them since childhood. When you can be completely honest and intimate with yourself, *then* you will have the courage to be completely intimate and bare your soul to the one you love.

Whether you are sharing your favorite music or a fear you have, being completely yourself is truly the only way to go if you desire a deep, long-lasting romantic relationship. Never just say things that you think your partner wants to hear. Speak honestly at all times concerning every facet of your life and preferences.

The love agreement of honesty also requires that you speak from your heart. Heart-to-heart communication is vital in your relationship. In fact, the only way you will ever be able to sustain a lifelong relationship is with complete honesty and transparency every day and night for the rest of your life.

To create a safe environment with the one you love to be completely honest with you is to say, "I want you to know that you can tell me anything. Any fears or insecurities you have, anything that is bothering you, and I will listen with an open heart and mind. I will be your best friend, and together we will help each other grow and evolve."

If your loved one said the above to you, how would you feel? Probably elated! I am positive you would feel so grateful. Take this first love agreement and create a safe haven for yourself where it is safe for you to uproot, verbalize, and transform anything unpleasant that you feel so you can become your own best friend. That is the only way you can be best friends with the one you love. That is the only way you can nurture your relationship, so it is always safe to be completely you—and the same is true for your partner.

Everyone must feel safe to share whatever is unpleasant deep within themselves in order for relationships, romantic or otherwise, to blossom. Sharing every positive quality that you see and experience with the one you love is equally vital. Let him or her know every adoring, lovable quality that you admire. Show gratitude for every little thing he or she says and does for you. Say, "I love you for exactly who you are!"

Everyone wants to feel loved, accepted, and appreciated. If you are with someone you deeply love, let him or her know *why* you are deeply in love. This positive infusion of pure, heart-centered appreciation works miracles in a relationship. Never let a day go by without saying, "I love you." Share your support for their progress. Share your encouragement if they are going through a rough time. Say, "Babe, I'm totally here for you, and I know this difficulty is temporary and will be behind you very soon."

Being an honest support system is crucial. Being your partner's best friend is what true honesty is all about.

CHAPTER 2

❧

THE LOVE AGREEMENT TO BE BEST FRIENDS

Don't you want your loved one to be your dearest and best friend? They also want to experience the same thing from you.

Being best friends means you are completely there for each other. You treat the one you love with the utmost care, respect, and compassion, and you always have their back.

Being best friends is crucial when you have committed to someone for life. It is paramount that you both know you can count on each other when the chips are down, as well as celebrate each other's victories in life. Being best friends requires gentleness from the bottom of your heart.

There are zero games when you are best friends. This means that there are zero manipulative tactics to get what you want or to try to control the other person.

Being best friends means you can trust each other from the bottom of your heart and soul, and you always treat each other with kindness, exactly as you would treat another best friend, except the bond in a lifelong partnership goes much deeper.

You can see all the gifts, talents, and abilities in your loved one, and you are a source of unconditional love and acceptance for them. You are there to help in any time of need. You are on the same page, and even more so, you are both on the same letter of the same word on that same page. You go out of your way to be a source of compassion and cheer. You both agree that the foundation of the greatest love relationship is a true and complete best friendship.

When your loved one needs reassurance, they don't have to ask you for it because, as their best friend, you freely give it. Saying "I believe in you" is a powerful statement, and it can spur the one you love on to greatness if they have been going through challenges. You show total care in the most loving way toward each other twenty-four seven.

Being best friends means there are no ego games or control tactics, and there is never abuse in any form. On the other hand, if there is a total lack of respect, the presence of control issues or abuse, and a complete lack of deep care about your loved one, I can guarantee this relationship will one day become history. Nobody wants to be with someone that is not their dearest best friend. This requires a total heart-centered commitment on both of your parts to eradicate anything, any words and actions, that a best friend would never say or do. It is a complete overhaul in the love department to ensure that your relationship lasts a lifetime if this is what you truly desire.

If you don't want to treat your loved one with complete care, compassion, respect, and gentleness, then do him or her a favor and move yourself out of the relationship. Nobody wants to be with an adversary. Every human being wants to experience true love, and the foundation of *true* love is a best friendship.

You both have to feel secure enough that you can tell each other anything and know that whatever you say is acknowledged with love. If you can't speak openly and honestly to each other and have your feelings acknowledged with love, care, and compassion, then this is not a true love relationship, and it won't last the test of time.

If you are not currently in a relationship, make sure your next one develops the foundation of a best friendship *before* the passion.

If you want a lifelong partner on the soul level, you must treat the one you love with all of the care and respect in the world. Additionally, this needs to be a requirement that you have in your relationship that you are learning about each other and sharing your feelings and experiences always with an open heart. Heart-centered compassion and care go a very long way. In fact, they are truly the only ways your relationship can flourish.

Whether you're revamping this area in your current relationship or starting fresh in a new one, make sure you discuss the importance of a best friendship where it is safe to express the times you each feel down and uplift each other until a breakthrough is made. You have to be your partner's very best friend and only allow yourself to progress into a romantic relationship when your partner treats you like a best friend.

Express how vital the foundation of a best friendship is. Then show it in every way possible. It must be equal. Your partner must do the same with and for you—only then your relationship will blossom and grow in profound ways over time. You will experience deep trust and excitement and eventually bliss when you both know you are always truly there for each other. This dynamic creates a deep sense of security that will continue to build over time, and you will both be so glad that you each invested your heart and soul to truly be there for each other, respect each other, and treat each other like platinum and diamonds and, even more, as the once-in-a-lifetime love that no difficulty can ever extinguish because you will both know every day that you are truly there for each other for the rest of your lives.

CHAPTER 3

໔

THE LOVE AGREEMENT FOR POSITIVE RESOLUTION

Positive resolution means the refusal to be negative. It means that no matter what you and your loved one are facing, there is a positive resolution at hand, and all you need to do is speak it and ask for it from whatever name you give to your Higher Power, be it God, Creator, Higher Self, Divine Intelligence, or whatever you personally understand this name to be.

You see, when we go through difficulties, we might not be aware at that time that they are, in fact, a blessing of some form in disguise. In 2010, I had best-selling books and client sessions packed into my schedule. I was very happy and "on top," so to speak. Then, out of the blue, I broke my left foot getting off my living room couch. After that, I began to have female bleeding twenty-one days out of each month. I had to cancel all of my client sessions. I was weak, depleted, and bleeding. I also had a serious bad habit of spending every penny I made on nonessential items—more and more boots, handbags, jewelry, and watches. I was guided from within to stop all nonessential spending, but I of all people did not listen to that inner guidance. I thought, "Why should I have to stop buying things I like with my own hard-earned money? I'm not using any credit cards." So I had to learn the hard way, and I shared many lessons from this time in my life in my book *The Rush to Spend*. I came home from the hospital in October 2010 to an eviction notice on my penthouse door. I had to move into my car.

For eight solid months, I lived the most humiliating existence in my SUV, feeling subhuman without a trace of dignity. I have to admit that although that was a horrible experience, I learned how to manage my finances and only buy what is necessary. It was actually, in hindsight, one of the best things that happened to me because that lesson is saving me for the rest of my life. I only buy what is truly necessary. This is the silver lining behind that dark cloud.

Perhaps you may also be going through a very difficult time. Remember that challenging circumstances never arise to punish you—they are there to strengthen you. They help you grow into your best possible version of yourself. They also bring out the incredible gifts you have from within and allow you to start viewing yourself as a blessed person. You have gifts that only *you* came into this life to share in a way that is as unique as your fingerprint.

No matter what you are facing, it is preparing you for greatness.

Here is the key: stop all complaining. Stop putting yourself down, and *never* put down the one you love that you are in a romantic relationship with. For that matter, never put down anyone in any way. Stop all negative talk.

You create your future by speaking greatness over your life. Your words have tremendous power! Everything you say is a command you are giving to the universe to deliver *exactly what you are speaking*. You may not feel so great inside. You may feel down and alone. But with your higher power, you are never alone.

Having a positive resolve also means coming to a peaceful resolution with the one you love over any matter weighing on your heart and mind. Anyone can complain. And all that does is bring us more to complain about—again, the universe is going to deliver to you everything you speak.

Sit down or get on the phone with the one you love, and come to a positive agreement over anything you feel upset about. The key is to speak from your *heart*. This cannot be a battle of ego and who is wrong versus who is right. It is about pure, heart-centered sharing and a willingness to come to a peaceful, positive resolution every step of the way.

If you are being abused in any way, including verbal put-downs, mental abuse, being told everything is your fault, or if you are being hit—this is physical abuse. When you let your loved one know that you are never going to take abuse again, take note of their reaction. If he or she agrees to never abuse you again, this is awesome. However, if he or she tells you that it's all your fault and you "made them" abuse you, the *only* thing you must do is completely exit this abusive relationship.

You must have a positive resolve to only allow yourself to be treated in a way that is loving, caring, kind, and supportive.

When you realize that you are being abused and nothing is changing, it is your own personal responsibility to yourself to exit the relationship as quickly as possible. Ask for help. Open up, and share what is happening, and you will be amazed at the positive help that is sent to you. You are never truly alone. One friend may say, "You can stay with me until you can get your own place."

You must *decide* the rest of your life is going to be the best of your life and refuse to allow any negative person or situation to keep you down. It is time that you have the inner resolve to bring you a guarantee from the universe that where you set your sights is exactly where you are headed. Stop *all* complaining immediately and instead state to yourself the real facts that "I am headed for greatness, and I am using every lesson and every tear to share with others who are going through the same situation to uplift both myself and countless others." You can share it in a book or a video if you want to help others learn from your lessons.

Share where you failed and what you learned. Share how having a positive resolve truly creates miracles in both your life and everyone else's. The ancient saying "Do unto others as you would have them do unto you" is crucial.

A pivotal dynamic is to forgive everyone who has ever hurt you. The forgiveness is not for them—it is to free you from the toxic emotions of anger, suffering, and bitterness.

If anyone has hurt you, take the high road. Walk away with dignity, and never do anything to hurt them in return. Allow the universe to deliver karma. Trust me on this one—the universe will deliver far more than you could ever do on your own.

So what does all I have shared so far in this chapter have to do with a love agreement?

Love of self; love for your partner, either present or future; love of your life; love for the gifts on the other side of your struggles—they are all interwoven like a tapestry. Your resolve to remain positive despite appearances to the contrary is so crucial, I cannot stress this enough. It will take you from the bottom to the top in every area of your life. The kind of relationship you have in your love life must be infused with positivity every single day and night.

As you begin to turn your words around, you will notice that your life begins to match your words. Make your words only the best. This is what you deserve, so claim it. Give thanks for it all in advance.

Know that no other person can "complete" you. You were born complete. Your loved one can bring you tremendous joy, and you can share your joy with the ones you love. However, never place all of your being, worth, and value in another person's hands. You were born worthy and valuable.

Have the positive resolve to remind yourself of this every day. If you need a major boost in self-esteem, look into the mirror, and twice a day tell yourself three good qualities you have based on your observable actions. For example, if you held the door open for an elderly person with a walker, you can look into your eyes and say your name, then say, "When you held the store door open for that elderly person, that was so kind, caring, and compassionate of you."

When you tell yourself three good qualities based on your observable actions, the ego cannot dispute it because it is fact.

When you do this once during the day and once before you go to bed at night, it will create a bonding experience you will feel deep within yourself. You will start to become your own best friend. This is crucial because if you are *not* your own best friend from the inside out, you will continue to seek validation from others, and it will never feel like it is enough.

I did the mirror dialogue for two solid years, 1994 to 1996. It was assigned to me by a highly spiritually evolved man named Bill Burns in Los Angeles. Bill has passed away, yet his sharing with me continues to have a positive rippling effect as I share this mirror dialogue with you. It really works!

Give yourself a pat on the back for *any* positive thing you do. Start to become your own best friend so you will only allow the best and most positive people into your life. If you are around complainers, your life will continue to look like one huge complaint.

You only want a positive life, and you only want the same for your love relationship. Share this from your heart so you and your loved one get on the fast track to an amazing life.

Bring the highest and most powerful forces in the universe into your life because we truly cannot do it all on our own. We all need positive divine help and support to create the best life you can fathom. When you do this, you will come to find that the words you speak, the support you receive from God by whatever name you use, and the resolution to only be positive will result in a life and love relationship that exceeds your wildest dreams.

Count on it because it *is* yours once you declare it to be so. Declare it every day and watch how perfectly everything unfolds for your highest good and the highest good of the one you love.

CHAPTER 4

&

THE LOVE AGREEMENT FOR ATTENTION, AFFECTION, AND PASSION

The love agreement for attention, affection, and passion covers a myriad of areas, so let me start with attention.

Giving your loved one positive attention can be verbal, as in saying how much you appreciate your loved one or all the qualities you love about them. Showing and verbally expressing gratitude for every positive thing they and do is crucial to maintaining a healthy relationship. The more you give attention and express gratitude for the positive things they do, the more they will feel appreciated.

No matter how small the act of kindness is, be it helping you in the house or sending you a loving text message, your positive reaction ignites the love in their heart for you, and all they will want to do as a result is give you more to express your gratitude about.

Show attention by writing loving notes, dedicating a love song, or sending flowers or a gift. This expression of positive attention will do wonders to keep the flame of love not only ignited but bursting with gratitude from the one you love.

Affection is direly needed in relationships. A hug, holding hands, touching their face, and sharing how much you love them will keep the flames of true love burning no matter how many decades you have been together. It is crucial. Touching in a loving way on a daily and nightly basis is something every human being loves to feel. We all love to feel loved. Expressing your physical affection creates more bonding. It creates a dynamic that fuels a deeper love.

Never, ever take your loved one for granted. If you feel like you are being taken for granted, try showing more love by way of physical attention and stopping all nagging and complaining. I cannot stress this enough. Turn it all around by expressing your love in every way you possibly can.

Passion is the highest physical form of expressing and showing true love. Ignite the passion in your relationship, and it will take on a beautiful dynamic. Passion can be shown by deep kissing or holding each other, and where that goes is completely up to you both as a couple united in the deepest love.

Passion in or out of bed is a sacred act of love. Passion can be shown in any way your heart and imagination desire to express it. No matter how you do it, do it from the bottom of your heart and soul on a daily basis as best as you can and with the pure desire to bond more deeply with your loved one.

Far too many couples let their attention, affection, and passion wear off after years have passed. If this has happened in your relationship, one kiss, one touch, or one act of physical expression can turn years of a stale relationship back into a deeply loving, passionate one.

This must be shown every single day. Your partner will thrive on your love, and they will express their own in return. This is a dynamic that every human being craves.

Some couples have let all the affection and passion die, and they wonder why their spouse exits the relationship. Make sure from this day forward you make a new commitment to your loved one in actions first backed up by expressing loving words. This will keep your relationship fueled by love and chemistry, and the passion will continue to grow into your old age.

Be playful in expressing your attention, affection, and passion. It's OK to be sexy with the one you are in a deeply committed union with. Passion, sex, touching, love making, and verbalizing yourself in a playful, loving way will ignite sparks that may have become dormant in your love life.

Make today a fresh start. Surprise your loved one with a new sense of playfulness, a new sense of excitement, and a new dynamic of physical pleasure, and they will be so deeply grateful to you that you will see a renewed spark of love in their eyes. You will feel a refreshed sense of playful yet deeply loving bonding. This, if practiced daily, will awaken a revived sense of delightful adventure in your love relationship.

However you do it, make sure that you do, because every romantic relationship needs this in every area, in every way. It will seal your relationship at an extremely deep level. I can promise you that showing and expressing all your love, attention, affection, and passion will bring your relationship the greatest rewards that will last for the rest of your lives.

CHAPTER 5

❧

THE LOVE AGREEMENT FOR CELEBRATION

Celebration cannot just be reserved for birthdays and holidays—it must be expressed every day.

Just like special plants need water every day, so too does your love life. You must show in many little ways how much you love and adore your partner, be it song dedications, love notes, text messages and quotes, hugging, kissing, and verbally expressing how much your partner means to you, and you need the same from your partner. This is nurturing your love life and keeping it alive.

Have you ever felt like you were starving for love and appreciation? I have, and it's a horrible feeling. To always feel taken for granted and never truly shown deep and profound love is a miserable way to live in a romantic relationship.

I can also share with you that when I was shown in many ways how much he loved me, and as I did the same for him, our love blossomed so profoundly. We felt completely excited and cherished. This is crucial in a relationship—to say thank you for the big and small things. To feel and express genuine love in a myriad of ways keeps the flames of love burning bright. It makes us feel special, as we all deserve to feel.

This is something that cannot be taken or demanded for with a loved one, it can only be given. However, a heart-to-heart talk about the importance of celebrating your love with your loved one can do wonders for your relationship.

I want to keep this chapter positive; however, if you are with someone who never shows you how special you are, never expresses their deep love for you, or just leaves you starving for the love you need to be expressed, perhaps you may be with the wrong person. Not everyone is a romantic at heart, yet every person loves to feel admired and even treasured. Every person loves to feel love and loves to feel special to their loved one. I say this to you with great respect: if your loved one is working and is far from home, still express your love and celebrate your love in every way you possibly can.

What will happen if you are not being shown how much you matter to your loved one is you will begin to wonder if there is someone else on this earth who *will* show you how much you mean to them.

You will wonder if there is someone else who will celebrate you and your love together. This is a huge reason many couples part ways. They feel like they are totally taken for granted. Yet this can be turned around in one moment if you sincerely love the one you are with.

Celebrating the qualities you cherish in your partner is desperately needed every single day, just like the special plant I mentioned earlier. Write a love letter. Put a love note somewhere in the house to surprise your loved one. Dedicate to them a love song or a fun song or a passionate song, send loving text messages, open your heart. When you feel love shown to you all the time, it ignites your love and appreciation that will cause you to want to reciprocate in any way you can.

Celebrate your love every single day and night. Tell your loved one how much you appreciate them and how much they mean to you. Never, ever neglect your loved one and starve them for their need to be loved and appreciated. Never let a day go by that your deep love is kept silent. Always, as long as you want to be in this relationship, tell your loved one about the qualities they have that you admire. Say, "Thank you for being so awesome!"

I know this works wonders and causes the bonds of love to grow deeper and stronger. Just when you think you couldn't possibly love your partner more, they do or say something that goes to your heart and soul that causes your love to deepen. That is why there is the saying "I love you more and more each day." It is because love *does* grow deeper every day, and when this happens, your loved one will never stray away from you.

This is also part of the standards that are needed in your love relationship, to be with someone who has a loving and romantic side that matches yours. If you feel completely taken for granted, you may need to have a serious talk with your partner and share how you feel. Ask them how they feel about expressing love if their style is different from yours so you can both reach a middle ground of understanding. This will help greatly.

Celebrating love is like breathing. We can't be our best in a relationship when we are starving for true love, so make this promise to yourself that you will celebrate your partner. You can even talk to your partner about this chapter and see how they feel about celebrating love.

If you are in the beginning of a new relationship, definitely talk about how you like your romantic side to be expressed, if you do at all. Some people are closed off and don't like expressing love. If their style matches yours, you'll be fine. However, if their style is the opposite of yours, then you cannot change the basic nature of another person. Some people are romantic at heart, and some people just do not like all the romance and celebrating their love.

There is no judgment here at all. It's all about the basic nature of a person, including you. Be with someone who has the same style of celebrating so you never feel starved for loving attention. Express your desires, and at the same time, *always* express your appreciation for your loved one even if it is not in a romantic way.

However you celebrate your loved one and your love, make sure you do so that you can keep the love shining brighter, making you feel so grateful to have such an admiring partner. Your partner needs to be equally adored from the bottom of your heart.

CHAPTER 6

❧

THE LOVE AGREEMENT FOR ZERO ABUSE AND CONTROL

The title of this chapter may be blatant about the necessity for zero abuse and control, yet in my own life and in the lives of many people I have worked with, abuse and control were dominant in the relationship.

Verbal abuse, put-downs, and degrading comments hurt a lot. Calling someone degrading names destroys their self-esteem and inflicts deep pain that reaches the soul level.

When you have a partner that feels more like your adversary, your enemy; when you don't feel safe because you are being abused—this is a crucial time to seek help to exit the relationship.

If you are ever hit, pushed, kicked, smacked, or sexually hurt, this is the time you call 911. You are not in this life to be abused and controlled.

Control is when your partner watches your every

move as if you are living in a prison with twenty-four-hour video surveillance. If you're "not allowed" to have any personal time to yourself or if you are being watched constantly, this is the control you must free yourself from.

People who are abusive and controlling have very low self-esteem, and everything that is "wrong" is always made out to be "your fault."

Every human being deserves to live free to express him- or herself, to live with personal freedom and dignity, to never be put down, insulted, and made to feel like yesterday's trash.

No matter how you experience abuse and control, it is vital to your life and to your safety that you free yourself from it.

On the other hand, if you have been feeling insecure and have been monitoring your partner, you must do everything you can to raise your own self-esteem and to learn how to love yourself, because with true love there is zero abuse and control.

Allow no one to ever abuse you or control you. Yes, you can walk away. You can ask for help so you are safe to live free from harm.

This is the love agreement that can actually prevent a life-or-death situation. If you feel you are in harm's way or if you are experiencing abuse in any form, it is time to confide in someone in the medical field who can call the police and help you exit the relationship safely.

I actually experienced this in my own life. I was ill and married to a violent alcoholic. One day I had to go for thyroid biopsies, as the doctors thought I had thyroid cancer. I suddenly opened up to the nurse and let her know that my then-husband was starving me and not buying me food. I was forbidden to drive his car. I was trapped and scared to death.

She then said, "I'll be right back." She was gone for a few minutes and returned to me in the medical testing facility. She told me that she called the police because, as a medical professional, she had to report any abuse to the police if she felt a person's life was in danger. The police told me that I could only go back home if my then-husband would not be at home so I could get my belongings and leave. I literally ran for my life with my suitcase and laptop, and I was able to escape. I felt so grateful that the nurse called the police. I knew I was in deep danger and I had to leave.

So I am sharing this with you only because I have been there myself. I know how scary it is. The greatest thing was that I was able to finally leave California and return to Florida. After eight months, I filed for divorce. Then on my grandma Rose's one hundredth birthday, the judge in the courthouse granted me a divorce. I literally had a new lease on life. I knew that was a sign for me from the universe that I would heal and make a fresh start, and I did.

So I encourage you from the bottom of my heart and soul to exit *any* relationship where you are in danger because on the other side of your exit is a wonderful, loving, freeing, fantastic new life with the real opportunity for true love to enter and stay in your life for as long as you live.

I promise you that once you leave the abuse, you will restore to your true, vibrant self and you will flourish in every way, every day for the rest of your profound, incredible life.

CHAPTER 7

❧

THE LOVE AGREEMENT TO BE
EACH OTHER'S HAPPY PLACE

It is so important in a romantic relationship to know that when the chips are down, when anything upsetting happens, and when you or your loved one feels down that you can count on each other to be your comfort, joy, and reassurance that everything is going to be OK and to know with absolute certainty that you have each other to turn to as your happy place from the rest of the world.

Both you and your partner are your backup, your cheering squad, your comfort, and your joy all throughout your lives. No matter what storms or circumstances occur, you have each other as your happy place. You never ever tear each other down or put each other down in any way. You show the love and gratitude toward each other. You are a source of unfailing support and protection from the rest of your world.

Your home is also your happy place. The one place on earth you can always be exactly who you are and can show one another how much you mean to each other. When your passion and love are shown every day and night and when you know with absolute certainty that you are completely devoted to each other and are always there with loving arms and even a shoulder to cry on if you need it, you do in fact have a happy place in each other's arms.

Any insecurity you may feel is met with loving reassurance. Any doubts you may have either about your own self or your partnership are literally loved away. You feel immeasurable love both for your own selves and for each other. You help each other overcome personal growth challenges to become your own highest expression of yourselves in this lifetime.

Being each other's happy place means you have each other as your dearest and best friend twenty-four seven. All of your cares and worries are met with the utmost love that is so true and so deep, you both know without any doubt that you have finally found the one person on the planet who is solely meant for you.

You create fun together both inside and outside your home. You laugh together. You have passion in bed. You delight and surprise each other in fun, unique, and exciting ways.

If you have a lot of physical chemistry, your deep love and passion for each other are shown every day or night or both so you feel all of the love and excitement both on the physical level and in the depths of your heart and soul.

You greet each other with playful gestures. You take passion and playfulness to a whole new level, always creating new ways to express your love and physical chemistry.

You both make your relationship filled with so much love, excitement, and pleasure that neither one of you would ever want to stray away.

You have found your forever person. You express in every way you can imagine how fun it is to be together. You are much more than a support system to each other. At the deepest level, you are the other half of each other's souls.

As one another's happy place, you know you can bring up any topic that may be upsetting you and you will be met with full support from your partner with an open heart and mind to clear anything up in the most loving, caring way possible.

All of this is what makes a relationship so profound that you are each filled with gratitude for each other, and you express this to each other both in words and actions every single day.

Talk about this with your partner if you need to create a new happy place together. It can do wonders for your relationship. If you are with the right person, he or she will do everything possible to be your happy place, and you will do the same.

Go for it because the rewards and the depth of love will be so profound you will be filled with extreme gratitude that, in addition to the other nine love agreements in this book, only a happy place in your relationship can bring.

It is exciting and thrilling to know you have one soul who is always there for you. Be your partner's happy place. If you are with the right person, he or she will gladly be your happy place in return for the rest of your lives.

CHAPTER 8

❧

THE LOVE AGREEMENT TO KEEP OUR RELATIONSHIP BUSINESS PRIVATE

The one you are in a deep romantic relationship with deserves to have confidentiality with regard to anything that may upset you and vice versa. *You* deserve confidentiality as well.

Far too many couples complain about the one they are in a love relationship with to other people. All this does is create more drama, and yet, when you think about it, it does not do anything to create true harmony and a best friendship with the one you love.

It is vital to keep your relationship business private, especially if you are going through any upset. Why? Because the only way you can resolve any upset is when you discuss it with your partner and only your partner. When couples go through challenges and they discuss them with other people, those people will judge. Then when you resolve those challenges with your loved one, the people you have complained to only remember the bad that happened.

Being in a lifelong partnership requires real trust. One of the foundations of trust is confidentiality. You both deserve to keep your relationship business private, and this includes social media. Only share the good if you want to, such as an anniversary. The best thing to share on social media about your private relationship is nothing at all.

Every couple goes through challenges. It is nobody's business at all. When you both grow, evolve, and come to the other side of your challenges, you become a more solid and much stronger and love-filled couple.

If anyone asks you about your partnership, simply say that you love each other, period. You do not have to give a blow-by-blow account of the challenges you go through like a soap opera. Gossip is very dangerous! People *will* judge and try to find out more about your relationship, so when you keep it short and sweet and refrain from gossiping, your relationship will continue to strengthen as you both grow as individuals while you overcome your private challenges.

It is important for you to understand that all I have shared in this chapter pertains to the one true love you are going to spend the rest of your life with. If you are leaving a toxic, abusive relationship and you need loving support to help you until you exit the relationship, then confide in someone who will truly help you evolve and leave peacefully. A great rule of thumb is if you are staying in the relationship permanently, keep your relationship business private. If you are leaving an abusive relationship, do confide in a dear friend so you are not all alone.

What matters most in the area of your relationship business is that each of you is growing and evolving into your highest and best self. A romantic relationship is fantastic ground for you to experience such growth. You will find that as you grow as a couple and overcome your challenges together, there is a greater bond, a more solid foundation, and most of all, trust!

Be trustworthy by keeping anything you both go through solely between you and no one else. It is crucial to know that your partner is not gossiping about you behind your back and you are not gossiping about them either.

Trust is truly one of the most crucial aspects of a deep relationship. Keep your business private, and you will both bloom together without the opinions of others. Other people are not in your relationship, so keep matters of the heart quiet and confidential. By doing this, you can never go wrong.

Chapter 9

The Love Agreement to Stop All Complaints to Create the Best Future Together

Noticing what needs to be changed within your relationship must be done from the heart and in a loving manner. Complaining, nitpicking, and being sour and negative will never work in turning anything around that needs to be addressed.

Speak to your partner the way you would like them to speak to you. For example, "Honey, I noticed this, and from my heart, I'm asking if you would do or say this instead." This is loving, direct communication, and your partner will appreciate this approach just as much as you would.

Another facet of stopping all complaining is about the circumstances in your life. Every word you say is so powerful, it is like a megaphone telling the universe exactly what to bring more of to you in your life. When you complain, the universe brings you more to complain about because the universe is neutral, and your words continue to show up in your life exactly as the circumstances you are complaining about. Instead, try the approach of positive focus and the positive belief that your circumstances can, in fact, turn around to your delight.

I have done this in my own life, and I noticed that when I stopped all complaining, everything started to get better.

Whether or not you believe in God, Source, Creator, Divine Intelligence, or simply the energy of the universe, everything is energy. When you create a decision of exactly what you truly want to manifest in your life and with your partner and when you speak only positively about it, never again uttering a negative word despite current temporary appearances, the universe has no choice but to deliver only the positive words you speak.

No matter how long you may have been experiencing a setback or a situation, it can indeed turn around in a split second, and it does for so many people around the world who have a positive mindset and refuse to utter a negative word.

A great part about "being realistic" is remembering a time when you saw any person in the world go from being the underdog to being in victory.

I'll share a deeply personal example from my own life. In 1998 I had shared custody of my two precious children, and it was my turn to enjoy their Christmas break with them. Three days before Christmas, I had thirty dollars to my name, no Christmas tree, and no presents for my children. I refused to allow the "reality" of my situation keep me down. I strongly visualized a giant Christmas tree in my living room and presents for my children filling the entire living room. I said to myself, "I am going to give my children the best Christmas they have ever had." Filled with the deepest love for my children, I then went and sold advertising with the strongest determination. I sold a lot of advertising. As a result, I bought an eight-foot Christmas tree and gift wrapped eighty-one presents for my children and spread them all around the tree and all over the living room. When I picked them up and brought them home, they lit up with huge smiles on their faces. They and I were ecstatic. It was one of the greatest memories of my life that showed the power of visualization and positive talk despite appearances to the contrary. It was indeed the best Christmas we ever had.

This is what I am trying to convey to you. Once you start to form an agreement with yourself and your partner about all of the great things you want to experience together and all of the areas you want to see turn around in the most positive ways, and when you both agree to only speak with faith that aligns with your believe system, you will be amazed at how your circumstances are going to turn around completely.

You can be the "lucky couple" who has it all: love, health, fidelity, prosperity, and all of your dreams and desires as to how you want to show up in this world—it is all possible. I would even venture to say that not only is it possible, if you keep being positive, it is inevitable.

The beginning of your future starts right now. If your partner has been stating every negative aspect of life they see, then it is time to have a heart-to-heart talk about the laws of the universe. What you say comes back to you as your reality. This is crucial if you want to create a life that is extremely positive in every manner.

Speaking and visualizing positive things until they manifest is the truth. It is not just an airy-fairy affirmation—when you say, "Prosperity is chasing us down," prosperity finds its way to you. When you declare that you only have the very best life you came here to live and that "how" is completely up to the universe, you will let go of the "how" and embrace sudden, inspired ideas. This book was a sudden, divinely inspired idea. Many books are. If you see the success in your mind, feel it in your heart, and get so excited about it that you truly believe it is in fact becoming a reality, it will become a reality.

I am no different than you. We all go through challenges and difficult periods because we all have learning, growing, and evolving to do.

Your relationship can take on the highest expression of your combined love fueled with a positive purpose to bring each of your talents and gifts into this world. Your relationship itself is one magnificent aspect of this manifestation. The other part is how you both decide you want to experience the rest of your life together, how much of a difference you both want to make in any capacity that ignites each of your hearts.

Eliminating every negative word is as crucial to your life moving forward as oxygen is to keeping you alive.

If you both need to get unstuck, you have to only speak with positivity. If you want to see a specific challenge turn around, start speaking, visualizing, and saying, "It is now turning around."

Remember that you are a very powerful cocreator with respect to every facet of yourself and your life.

Never say another negative word! If you have weight to lose, stop calling yourself fat. Start saying,

"I am now getting my gorgeous, skinny figure back," while you begin a super healthy diet. The months are going to go by, and the day will come when you are skinny again. I went through this same challenge. I kept picturing my old model figure back and stayed on a strict diet because I wanted my reflection in the mirror to match my ideal figure.

Stop putting yourself down! Start calling yourself a winner, a pure soul who is here to live a fantastic life. Start speaking victory along with gratitude for every area of your life that you want to turn around.

There is something consistent about every underdog who becomes a champion and every couple who overcomes their challenges together, and this is fierce determination, a tunnel-vision focus backed by positive words and actions and refusing to allow any negative words or energy to have the power to affect them. It is all positive focus backed by positive action.

When you and your partner turn your back on all complaints because they have obviously gotten you nowhere and when you make the love agreement to only speak with positive words and have a positive mindset combined with positive actions, you will see everything turn around no matter how long there may have been challenges in your life.

This is a wake-up call because I deeply want you to experience your best self, your best relationship, and your very best life on every level. Only positive thoughts, words, and actions can achieve this, and this is true for every human being alive.

The universe knows how to connect all the dots, the people, and the sudden break that you need. Your job is to keep believing in your *result*.

The same is true for every aspect of your dream life. Cut out a picture, write your goals down with pen and paper, affirm it, and stay positive about it.

Remember this saying: "When I speak it, the universe repeats it."

That literally just poured through me from God. When you speak it, the universe repeats it. So only speak what you want to see manifest. Share this phrase with your partner so you can both be double positive combined with all you both want to see and experience in your life.

Remember how powerful you are, how much truth your words create in your life. Stay completely away from *all* negativity. Remain in a positive mind-set and mouth-set, speaking only that which you wish to see the universe repeat in your life.

When you speak it, the universe will bring it.

CHAPTER 10

੨੪

THE LOVE AGREEMENT TO FULLY AWAKEN FOR PROFOUND TRANSFORMATION

What does it mean to fully awaken? It means that when your own intellect cannot figure out a solution to a problem or a better way to relate to the one you love, you instead awaken your sixth sense, the higher part of your mind that can receive immediate answers to resolve any conflict that may occur, by turning to the highest source in the universe by whatever name you personally use, be it God, Creator, Higher Self, Higher Consciousness, or Divine Intelligence.

By awakening your sixth sense, you are utilizing all of yourself, and as a result, you are no longer depleted by relying solely on the five-sense intellect when real transformation is what you desire in any aspect of your life, especially your own personal growth and the growth of your relationship. How to awaken comes from a deep desire in your heart to do so. This is what activates your higher consciousness to God, or your Higher Self.

When you are going through a problem in your life or in your relationship, did you know that you can receive the perfect solution within *minutes*? Take out paper and a pen and simply write "Dear God" or "Dear Higher Self" and your question, such as, "How can I resolve this conflict my loved one and I are having? Please guide me!" Then take five deep breaths, and you will notice words flowing into your mind in the form of an answer. Write down every word without censoring anything. Then at some point, the guidance will come to a natural finish. Reread everything you brought through, every word, at least three times. You will be amazed exactly like I have been at the clarity, the truth, the perfect solution, and the real transformation the guidance provides.

I have been sharing this process for the past twenty years as of the time of writing this book. The people I have shared this process with spanned 191 countries, and so many people were elated that they were, in fact, receiving higher guidance that was so on point and so transforming their problems were resolved within minutes or within one hour.

No matter what challenge you are facing, there really is a higher solution, and all you have to do is write it down. When you turn to this process and experience firsthand how incredibly transforming it is, never again will you try to figure it out on your own. That is why you do have a higher consciousness, and you can utilize this process to transform any aspect of yourself that you want to turn around, as well as any aspect of your relationship.

Relationships do bring up core, soul-level issues of growth we came into this lifetime to make. My question to you is this: Is your partner also willing to receive the higher answers for their own transformation as well? You will only know the answer by asking them.

If every couple turned to this pure, free process, all matters would be quickly resolved.

After decades of self-loathing and low self-esteem, I turned to this process when at one point in my life I didn't want to live anymore, and within five minutes, literally, I had a fresh lease on life with the new desire to not only live but to create a whole new life after experiencing deep injustice. It completely transformed me!

I can only share with you that if you have had a breakup and feel yourself hurting, this process will transform your pain and tears, and the higher perspective that our own personalities often cannot see while viewing everything from the five sensory intellect is completely turned around when we make use of this process.

Remember that in a romantic relationship you are not there to "complete" each other but instead to complement each other, living in harmony with one another, as each of you is already a whole and complete human being. This is the process that will ensure you are as whole and complete as you deserve to feel.

No matter what stage of the relationship you are in, you can turn to this process for immediate solutions and to awaken, and once you are awakened, you will continue to utilize all six of your senses by asking for and receiving the higher answers.

If all of humanity did this, earth would be a paradise and so would our relationships.

Utilize this process to receive the best solutions to any matter you and your partner are facing that you would like to see turn around. You will receive the higher answers, and they will amaze you.

If there is anything of the utmost importance I want to impress upon you, it is that by turning to God, or your Higher Self, you will truly come to know what a profound connection you really do have to the highest source of love, wisdom, and truth in the universe. You will know with absolute certainty that you are never alone, even if you may feel alone at times.

It is so vital that you do take this step to awaken so that you can receive the higher perspective so that you will never again be at a loss as to what to do or say, and you will never be at a loss for how to view any circumstance you go through. The higher reason we go through challenging circumstances is so that we can grow through them.

The fastest way to grow is by awakening your sixth sense. The fastest way to transform a relationship problem is by taking out a pen and paper, asking for the solution, and then writing down every word that flows into your mind. You will definitely grow! You will transform what used to plague you at lightning speed. When we are awakened and turn to our higher power for the answers, the answers truly reach the core of our mind, heart, and soul in ways that transform us and our lives. Turn to this process for any area of your life where you feel unhappy. You will receive the higher perspective that will definitely put a smile on your face.

I have shared much in this book regarding the ten love agreements that a romantic relationship needs to flourish. Our relationships can only flourish when each of us is flourishing as a whole and complete individual.

As I continue to utilize this process, it still amazes me. I only hope you, too, will turn to your higher self, God, or whatever name you personally use so that you thrive, your relationship thrives, and you become a walking example of living life in the best manner possible so people will start to ask you, "How did you turn it all around?" Give them the answer of awakening their sixth sense and turning to their pure higher power, their higher self, for the answers that transform the underdog into the champion, the lonely person into the thriving person, and the sad person into the delighted person.

This love agreement is one that you truly need to have with your own self, and you need a partner who is willing to awaken in order to truly have the best relationship each of you desires and deserves.

God, your higher self, is incredible with swift solutions that result in lightning-fast transformation. Utilize this process for the rest of your life. Share it with the one you love. You will both be amazed at how incredibly easy and swift this process is for turning anything around that is unpleasant.

Remember, you are never alone. Your higher power is always with you to transform tears to joy. It is unfailing, and this, my new friend, is what will transform every facet of your relationship and your entire life when you do utilize it.

About the Author

Barbara Rose, PhD most widely known as "Born to Inspire" is the bestselling author of thirty three books, a world renowned Higher Self Relationship and Life Transformation Expert, spiritual teacher, and transformational public speaker. Her personal growth and transformation shared with millions of people from every part of the world has endeared her to the masses as a pure, loving, and caring soul who shares by living example teaching humanity how to receive pure answers from God/Higher Self. Her ability to take the most difficult personal topics and bring through the solutions for herself and all has made her highly acclaimed work continuously shared globally with subscribers spanning 191 countries. Her official website is https://borntoinspire.com.

www.ingramcontent.com/pod-product-compliance
Lightning Source LLC
Chambersburg PA
CBHW030030290326
41934CB00005B/558